KABBALAH ON love

Distributed by Publishers Group West

KABBALAH ON

love

YEHUDA BERG

For further information:

The Kabbalah Centre
155 E. 48th St., New York, NY 10017
1062 S. Robertson Blvd., Los Angeles, CA 90035

1.800.Kabbalah www.kabbalah.com

First Edition
January 2007
Printed in USA
ISBN10: 1-57189-557-4
ISBN13: 978-1-57189-557-8

Design: HL Design (Hyun Min Lee) www.hldesignco.com

To my soul mate—my wife, Michal, you keep me steady;
you ground me and keep me real.

The gentle way you care for our life and our children,
opens my heart and makes me whole.

You define me. Without you, I am nothing.
I love you.

TABLE OF CONTENTS

Chapter Four

TRANSFORMATION:

FROM *NEED* TO *LOVE*

ACKNOWLEDGMENTS

To the people who make my life better each and every day: my parents, the Rav and Karen; my brother Michael; my wife Michal and our children; and my dear friend Billy.

Chapter One

what's love got to do with it?

LOOKING FOR WHAT?

Why did you pick up this book? What was it about the title or the subject matter that made you think this book was for you? I know, I know: Everyone wants to learn more about love. It can't hurt to have a little more insight into this sought-after phenomenon, right? But for you, it's personal. You want to know more about love because right now, in this moment, you're feeling a lack of it (or you did yesterday, or you will tomorrow), and you don't know why.

Maybe you picked up this book because . . .

- You're currently in a relationship that by all appearances is loving, yet you have a suspicion, deep in the recesses of your solar plexus, that something is missing. There are more than a few times when you feel disconnected from your partner, like two strangers passing in the night. A vague sense of sadness and uneasiness underlies your relationship. Everyone tells you how lucky you are to have found someone so wonderful; you smile and say the words that indicate you agree but wonder privately why good fortune feels so empty.

- Or perhaps your partner is someone who constantly undermines your sense of self-worth and takes advantage of your insecurities. The funny thing is that you've been here before—numerous times. In fact, you always seem to attract partners who manipulate, use, and hurt you. Your life feels like a heartrending country song, and you're starting to sense that you've been looking for love in all the wrong places for far too long. But you are plumb out of ideas for new places to look.

- Maybe all of this talk about relationships is becoming annoying because you aren't in a relationship, and haven't been for a while. At this point you'd settle for any partnership that even vaguely resembled love—or even fondness, for that matter. You'd be willing to make a world of compromises as long as you didn't have to be alone anymore. Or perhaps you're tired of sacrificing your standards, and you're ready to find your one true love—your unequivocal counterpart, your soul mate.

- Maybe your reasons for picking up this book have nothing to do with finding that ideal partnership, or improving the one you have. Maybe your reasons encompass a larger space than that. Perhaps you feel as though your social network is consistently letting you down. You feel as if you are giving nothing but love to your children, your parents, and your friends, but are receiving little in return. You want more from these relationships, but you don't know how to get it.

What if I told you that the reason you aren't getting whatever you're looking to find from love is that you are missing the point entirely? Would I offend you, or would I pique your interest? I'm shooting for the latter. Bear with me.

WHAT'S LOVE ALL ABOUT

It's no wonder that you are feeling a lack of love in what should be your closest relationships. It's because you've forgotten what true love is all about. So if you really want to find love—if you truly want to understand the emptiness that you feel—then you must remember this: To experience real love is to come face to face with the ultimate purpose of life. To achieve real love is to reacquaint yourself with you and the meaning of your own existence.

And here is the first kabbalistic secret concerning love:

The meaning of life and the meaning of love are identical.

See the problem? No one knows the meaning of life, which means that no one knows what true love is. When we know what life is all about, we will know what love is all about.

Now, if you're familiar with Kabbalah, perhaps you already have an intellectual understanding of your true nature, the purpose of life, and the true nature of love. But do you really know it on a gut level? If you did, you would not have picked up this book. If you've been learning Kabbalah for a while, it may be time to add a new dimension to your knowledge. And if you're new to Kabbalah, then strap yourself in for the ride—because your ultimate potential as a human being is about to be revealed!

What Exactly *Is* Love?

We throw the word love around quite a bit, don't we?

"I absolutely *love* grilled salmon," you say as you take a bite of your meal. Yet if you truly loved the fish, would you really be eating it? No; instead, you'd be working to protect the waters it breeds in. What you like is what the meat of the fish gives you—you enjoy its flavor and its texture. Your love has little to do with the well-being of the fish; it has everything to do with your dining experience.

"This country singer has the most wonderful voice. I just love him," you say. You've never met the singer, but you appreciate the acoustic attributes of his voice. *You* feel good every time you hear him sing. Again, your love has little to do with the other person and everything to do with you.

I'll bet you're starting to get the point.

The word *love* has become so overused that it has lost its meaning almost entirely. What we think love is, really isn't love at all.

So what does it really mean to love?

DECONSTRUCTING LOVE

Most dictionaries simply do not do justice to the word *love*. Definitions vary slightly, of course, but most describe love as a strong affection you feel toward another person—a pretty underrated assessment, to say the least.

Other definitions describe love in connection with sexual desire. The excitement barometer definitely skyrockets with the use of a phrase like *sexual desire*; however, such definitions still fail to tell the whole story.

Buried deep within the various definitions of the word love, we find this:

> *Unselfish, loyal, and benevolent concern for the good of another.*

Now we're getting a little warmer . . .

As this definition points out, true love has to do with the well-being of another human being. Did you notice the word *unselfish*? This word is critical, because when you really love someone, you remove your *self* from the equation. We'll talk about how to accomplish that a little later. In the meantime, let's do a quick exercise.

Defining This Thing Called Love

Think of someone important to you—someone very important, someone you love. Then read the following questions. Jot down your answers if you have a moment, or make a mental note, although I recommend writing as a tool here.

1. Why do you feel love for this person?

2. What makes this relationship a loving one?

3. How does this relationship make you feel?

Before you turn the page, please answer these questions.

Okay. How did that go? If you jotted your answers down, did you write things like:

- *She makes me happy.*
- *He really understands me.*
- *She supports me by providing for my needs.*
- *He makes me feel good about myself.*
- *She makes me feel needed.*
- *He accepts me for who I am.*
- *She makes me feel loved and cared for.*

If you answered this way, join the crowd. But take a look at how many times the word *me* shows up. Do you see what's wrong with this picture? These answers focus on how your partner is fulfilling your needs—how you are experiencing a lack of something and the way that person is filling it. According to Kabbalah, this is not love at all. But if it's not love, then what is it?

WHAT YOU'RE DESCRIBING IS *NEED!*

Bamboozled by Love

You've been led to believe that love is all about you and your needs! It isn't. In fact, need is the exact opposite of love. Need and love stand in total contradiction to each other.

This is a simple statement, but it can take a lifetime to grasp the profound principle at work here: 99.9 percent of the world believes they are in love when in fact they are in desperate need. This is why relationships inevitably break up. This is why we separate, divorce, and look for love in the all the wrong places. *We are trying to fulfill our own needs instead of trying to find love.*

But don't fret. This book is all about eliminating the confusion and misinformation surrounding the word *love*. In fact, we won't have to go far to get to the bottom of this tangle. Why? One reason:

> The entire secret of LOVE is revealed
> in the word itself.

This one four-letter word and the information it holds within tell us EVERYTHING we need to know.

A Look at the Numbers

Have you ever taken a sip of distilled water? Distilled water is free of all impurities. A process called distillation, which involves boiling the liquid and letting the steam condense into water again, filters out all contaminants. The end result is untainted, undeniably thirst-quenching H_2O.

Kabbalah uses a similar process to distill words down to their purest meanings; it's called numerology. Numerology teaches us that every word has a numerical value associated with it, based on the letters it contains. This value enables us to grasp and understand the inherent meaning of the word.

Make no mistake—numerology isn't like Sudoku, or crossword puzzles. It's far more than just an entertaining means of intellectual stimulation. No, numerology is a pathway to understanding existence at its most basic level. It's a powerful form of technology.

Remember when we discussed the various definitions of the word *love*? When human beings attempt to define love, they do so through the lens of personal experience. The benefit of numerology is that it leaves nothing to interpretation. When we use this kabbalistic tool, we are left with just the numbers—but the numbers tell the whole story.

In the ancient language of Aramaic,

- the word *love* has the numerical value of thirteen,

- the word *one* has the numerical value of thirteen,

- the word *care* has the numerical value of thirteen.

This is some pretty interesting stuff. Why? Because the number thirteen connects three ideas: *one*, *love*, and *care*. When words share the same value, an essential bond exists between them. When we experience oneness—when we truly care for another as we care for ourselves—this is love. It is the reunification of two halves of one soul.

Let's take this a step further. Thirteen is one above twelve. The number twelve is highly significant in Kabbalah. It represents all of our selfish needs (there's that word *need* again), which in turn are part of the predisposition given to us through the twelve signs of the zodiac at the moment of our birth.

What does all of this mean? Actually, it's pretty straightforward.

We create oneness with the other half of our soul and experience true love when we rise above our selfish traits.

That's it. Simple. Profound. Deep. Amazing.

But as grand as all of this sounds, why do we really want true love, as opposed to just filling our needs? Why have human beings sought out love since the dawn of human existence?

According to Kabbalah, love is the ultimate purpose of life, as we now know. But there is also a reason that finding love is difficult—why our true soul mate is so hard to find.

Chapter Two

the origins of love

IN THE BEGINNING

Tell me, tell me, tell me
Oh, who wrote the book of love?

I've got to know the answer:
Was it someone from above?

—THE MONOTONES

Why *is* it all about love? Why isn't *need* the purpose of life? Where did love come from? Why does it exist? These are questions that have been asked by poets, philosophers, and incurable romantics since the beginning of time. And the elusive answer to these questions is found at the very same place—the beginning of time!

To find love in your life, you must first discover love's true origins.

The Cause of All Causes

Long before the sun rose over the horizon and the Milky Way took its place in the cosmos—before the emergence of time itself—there was nothing but boundless energy. Kabbalists call this infinite flow of energy Light. Just as light radiates from the fireball that is our sun, spiritual energy—or Light—radiates from an all-powerful force known as God.

Ancient kabbalists wrote countless volumes of books that explore and explain the nature of this Light, and how our universe came to be. It's a sacred study that takes a lifetime to master. For the purpose of this book, however, I will try to simplify it and show you how it relates to the topic we are discussing.

The Light, the Vessel, and a Thing Called Love

In the beginning there was the Light. This Light consisted of pure, unconditional love. To be absolutely clear here, I'll repeat this:

Light = Love

One day, God decided to create an infinite soul—or a Vessel, in the language of Kabbalah—to receive this unconditional love. After all, real love cannot exist if there is no one to receive that love.

The infinite Vessel created by God included all the souls of humanity, which means you and me. The same way your body consists of trillions of cells, the One Soul, the One Vessel, was made up of trillions of souls.

The unconditional love that God gave the Vessel included every imaginable pleasure you can conceive of— and infinitely more. By all appearances, the Light and the Vessel were in perfect harmony, functioning as one divine organism that was sharing and receiving. But the union was not perfect; a vital component was missing. Can you guess what it was?

I'll give you a clue. It's the exact same thing that is missing when you are in a relationship in which you are the constant giver of your time, energy, and love while your counterpart is the constant recipient—or vice versa. Imagine for a moment that your lover spends every waking moment pampering you and catering to your every yearning. Sure, it might seem appealing at first, but that feeling would wear off fairly quickly, don't you think? You'd start to feel a little strange—maybe even a bit manipulated. Eventually, you'd crave a piece of the giving action yourself. It would be a bit like trying to play a game of catch in which you were able to catch the ball but couldn't throw it back to your partner. What would be the fun in that?

What makes this type of relationship so joyless is its lack of circuitry. Without circuitry, the relationship is finite. Without give and take, there is no space for love. Why? Because real fulfillment—real love—requires that each person play the role of *both* giver and receiver. It doesn't matter whether the relationship is between a parent and child or a husband and wife—existing in a constant state of receiving *or* giving simply loses its appeal after a while.

Imagine a man who is hugely obese and living at home with his mother. She brings platefuls of food to her son at every meal and supplies snacks in between. She's certainly giving, but is she really giving love? She might believe she is, but she is not. By encouraging his overeating, what she is really doing is a dangerous disservice to her son. Even though he is receiving everything he thinks he wants, is the son happy? No. And even though the mother is giving her son everything she thinks he wants, is she happy? No. Neither person in this scenario is fulfilled.

This is exactly what was going on between the Creator and the Vessel before time began. The Creator was sharing unlimited love with the Vessel, while the Vessel existed in a perpetual state of receiving. Imagine a ceramic mug filled with hot water. What happens to the mug? The mug takes on the nature of that which is poured into it, and becomes hot just like the water. In a similar fashion, the Vessel took on the characteristics of the Creator and developed a desire to share its love, too. It no longer wanted to be a passive recipient.

If you haven't figured it out, we are the Vessel. We, too, wanted to impart unconditional love to another being. But we couldn't. There was no other being to share it with. So we came up with a profoundly simple idea.

We resisted the Light. We told our Creator that we did not want to receive unconditional love unless we could also experience what it meant to share unconditional love.

So we asked God to withdraw, to retract a fraction of the love in order to create an infinitesimal empty space where we could experience the act of giving love unconditionally, just like our Creator.

God agreed. And that is when the Light vanished from the tiny space that we know as our vast universe. Something was still missing, however. Just as the

Creator had the Vessel to love, we too needed a partner to love. But there was no one. And that's when something remarkable took place. The Vessel purposely shattered into individual pieces. It splintered into countless sparks of individual souls to create the illusion of "other beings." Now, the souls would have someone to share unconditional love with—*each other!*

The Creation of Soul Mates

Each of these individual souls that were bound up inside the one Vessel had both a male and female aspect. When the Vessel shattered into pieces, all the male aspects separated from the female aspects. One soul became two halves. Thus male and female forces were born, each aspect representing half of what was once a single, unified soul.

THE MEANING OF LIFE

The ultimate objective of life is to reunite with our other half and become one again. This is the underlying reason behind our constant effort to seek out love. We feel incomplete. Lonely. Deep inside, we know something is missing. Finding our other half, our soul mate, is the key to finding lasting love and fulfillment. The question is how? How do we attract, find, and unify with our other half?

We achieve this by offering love unconditionally—with no strings attached, without any hidden agenda: loving for the sole sake of loving, the same way God does. The moment two halves of one soul offer love to one another unconditionally, they reunite into one. However, if two halves of one soul enter into a relationship based on need rather than unconditional love, then the relationship never grows and unification never takes place. You wind up with heartache instead of bliss.

So the solution sounds pretty simple, right? Just give love and you'll be happy. But once again, simple isn't the same as easy. Why not? For one thing, the thought of giving and not receiving feels as though you are ending up with the short end of the stick. All of our lives, we've been conditioned to feel pleasure from what we are receiving. Giving for the sake of giving may seem noble, but what's in it for me? Actually, everything is in it for you. But that truth has been hidden away. How? Why? And by whom?

Know Thy Enemy

To prevent us from recognizing ourselves in others (if we did, then sharing/loving would be easy), each spark of soul wears a costume called ego. The ego creates the illusion of difference, of *you* and *I*.

We have just identified your enemy in the game called life. This enemy, your ego, ignites feelings in you that oppose unconditional giving. Instead of loving absolutely, the ego compels you to receive absolutely, which you assist in by taking whatever you can. If we use our physical universe as a metaphor, the sun, which shares light, corresponds to your soul, your true self. A black hole in deep space, which only sucks in sunlight, corresponds to your ego. These are two opposite forces. One shares. The other takes. The part of you that shares is the *true you*. The part of you that wants only to take is the ego.

Before you find love, you must understand the following: The ego is an independent force that creates the illusion of difference by imbuing everyone with selfish desires—desires and needs that are the exact opposite of sharing and loving unconditionally.

What purpose does ego serve? Rising above the enemy—overcoming selfish desires—is how we learn to love unconditionally so that we may reunite with our soul mate and achieve the purpose of life, which is total joy and happiness. The same way you require resistance when building muscles with weights, you need an opposing force to resist when learning how to love unconditionally. The set of barbells is the ego.

Triumphing over the ego builds your love muscle; overcoming selfish traits is how you master the divine art of loving unconditionally.

This is why you are here. This is the meaning of life.

Enemy Tactics

The ego was devised to hide a profound truth: Giving arouses more pleasure than receiving. But you don't know this. You are not allowed to know this. The world was structured, by design, to reward egocentric behavior through immediate gratification. By contrast, unconditional love is designed to make you feel uncomfortable at first. It's hard. Difficult.

Make no mistake—when giving feels good, it's not real giving. In Kabbalah it's known as giving for the purpose of receiving, and it's really considered to be taking. True giving, true unconditional loving, must—absolutely must—be difficult to do. This is your clue that you are overcoming the ego.

So when you bemoan the fact that all the love you give is getting you nothing in return, you must embrace a harsh and difficult truth: You were sharing love for the purpose of receiving. And in doing so, you were not expressing your true divine nature. You were not achieving your life's purpose. God imparts love for no other purpose than to fulfill the needs of another. There is no thought, no consideration, and no calculation as to what that gift might generate in response. Hence, the moment you catch yourself wondering why your love is not being returned, you must recognize it's the ego and not the *true you* that is governing your behavior.

You see, the ego hates the whole idea of loving another without any regard for one's own desire. Every fear, every concern, every misgiving you have over the thought of offering your love and baring your soul solely for the sake of the other person is ignited by the enemy known as ego. When you follow its whims—when you allow the enemy to influence your behavior—you are on a path to short-lived relationships and loneliness. You are trading away lasting love that fulfills your heart and soul in exchange for short-term gratification.

Chapter Three

finding your
soul mate

SHARING VERSUS RECEIVING

Your soul is a spark of the original Vessel, as are the millions of souls with which you share this planet. The physical world came into being in order to provide you with boundless opportunities to fulfill your ultimate potential of sharing love, just as the Creator shares. The one thing that the Creator could not give us in the very beginning, we now have—we have the chance to offer our love to others.

But before you can offer your love to another, you must recognize your divine nature. God created you, which means that you yourself embody love; you embody Light. The very DNA of God is within your being. But you have another aspect: You have an ego. The ego works in opposition to your true divine self.

So you have an infinite capacity to receive *and* an infinite capacity to love. All too often, you fail to acknowledge your own Light. When you don't see your gift, your true self, you become desperate to take love from others in an attempt to satisfy your needs. This desperate need to take is motivated by your one and only enemy. When you exist in this state, you have nothing to offer those around you, and you move away from your true heart's desire.

Take, for example, a woman in an abusive relationship. Day in and day out, she exists in a constant state of receiving. Perhaps her partner mentally abuses her or physically mistreats her. Despite the cruelty of her undeserved punishment, she *takes* whatever her partner metes out. Why? Because she believes she has nothing to share. She sees no value in her own Light, her own love, so she exists in a desperate state of taking. Until she learns to connect with the love and Light inside of her, she will continue on the same painful course.

What's true for the abused woman is also true for you. Instead of focusing on taking, you must ask yourself, "What do I have to give?" What you have to give is truly extraordinary. You've just forgotten it, because you are covered in layers of obscurity. That's right, to prevent you from recognizing your self, the ego created many layers in order to gradually block out all the Light that radiates at your very core.

Layers Upon Layers

Like a brightly shining flashlight that has been dropped into a dark swamp, your Light still radiates brilliantly, but it is mired in muck. These layers of muck represent different aspects of the ego, which have been with you since the moment you were born under one of twelve astrological signs. The sign you are born under gives you your most dominant selfish traits. But make no mistake—your ego consists of selfish desires that emanate from every one of the twelve signs.

As I mentioned before, the ego and all of its layers are the ultimate enemy. Kabbalists acknowledge this by giving the ego a very specific designation: the Opponent. The Opponent is your reactive behavior, whether it is an egocentric impulse, a caustic comment, or a self-recriminating thought. It's an immensely powerful force whose sole purpose is to keep you from revealing the love that is at the core of your being. It aims to create chaos, darkness, and pain instead.

The Opponent is the voice that encourages you to withhold your love from others when you feel hurt, abandoned, and unloved. It is the voice that taunts, "You are not good enough to pursue a relationship with this person. He/she will surely discover all of your faults and run the other way." It is the voice that tells you that you are better off alone and that you are not worthy of love—not from others or from the Creator. It is the voice that tells you that no one on earth could possibly understand you or meet your needs, so you should try your best to fulfill them on your own. It is the voice that prompts you to protect your fragile self-worth at all costs.

What is the purpose of these painful thoughts? The Opponent designs them to keep you isolated and in an extremely needy state. And you know by now what happens when you are in this state: You become desperate to fill the void you feel inside. Instead of sharing your love unconditionally, the Opponent motivates you to do just the opposite—to receive or take unconditionally, leaving you feeling even less worthy than you felt before.

THE SECRET OF ONENESS

Despite the fear of loss and pain the Opponent creates, we've seen how defeating the Opponent, by resisting selfish desires, is the path to uniting with other souls.

Pause for a moment to think about that.

What does it really mean? What is oneness? Oneness means that you connect your soul to the other person's soul. In more practical terms, you let go of your selfish desires out of consideration for the other person's needs, and your partner does the same. Ordinarily, people interact through their egos. It's one ego talking to another ego. The ego serves only to create disunity and to promote separation, resulting in a state that we might call *two-ness*.

The Opponent creates a situation that allows us to *earn* oneness, to *earn* the gift of being just like God by sharing unconditional love. Without the Opponent's influences, we would be right back at square one—back to the joyless state of constant receiving.

The Opponent works tirelessly to make you forget that you really are the Light, the love. The Opponent aspires to make you believe instead that you are those layers that come between you and the Light. And that's precisely why we struggle in our relationships—we've all been duped into thinking that we are our ego. We've all been deceived into constantly receiving. We've all been fooled into believing that love is all about our own personal needs.

The Opponent has pulled off the biggest trick in the history of the human race!

And here's what happens when you and another soul enter into a relationship under this delusion:

Instead of two divine, loving souls interacting, layers are interacting with layers. And because both of you are drowning in layers of ego, you fail to recognize yourself in the other soul. It's no wonder you've never met your soul mate. You've both been wearing a costume the whole time. This keeps you from knowing who you really are. If you don't know it, you can't show it. And if you can't show it, how in heaven's name could your soul mate recognize you?

DECONSTRUCTING *SOUL MATE*

There's no denying that most of us aspire to meet our soul mate someday. But our idea of a soul mate is often misconstrued. When you think of a soul mate, what comes to mind? Someone who is a perfect fit for your personality, or someone with whom you never argue? Perhaps you imagine an individual who could anticipate and meet your every need before you can even ask to have it met. Wouldn't it be nice never to have to vocalize a thought, confront a fear, resist a temptation, or take a risk? You would never have to make amends for inappropriate behavior, because your soul mate would never provoke you. The innate beauty of your relationship would simply eliminate the need for difficulty or unpleasantness.

I hate to break it to you, but this scenario is most definitely *not* what it means to be in a soul mate relationship. A soul mate is not someone who makes your life a perpetually joyful walk in the park. Spiritually speaking, your soul mate is your other half—the aspect that makes your soul whole again.

Which leads us to the million-dollar question . . .

How can you find this elusive other half?

As human souls, we come into this world for the purpose of learning to share our love with others. Unconditionally. A task of this magnitude often requires that you labor for many lifetimes in order to reveal the amount of Light needed to elicit your soul mate. You see, it is only after you have worked diligently on eliminating your layers of ego, gradually learning how to share your love unconditionally, that you merit meeting your soul mate in this lifetime.

The Way to Genuine Soul Mate Love

Each soul embarks on a unique journey that gradually leads to its soul mate. That journey includes many relationships, and often many marriages over many lifetimes. The purpose behind every relationship is to bring you together with the right person for that moment—someone who can push your buttons all day long and incite reactions within you. Why? So that you are able to identify what it is you need to transform in yourself so that you can move another step closer to a true soul mate union.

As if finding your one true love weren't reason enough for you to seek out your soul mate, Kabbalah tells us that there is an even more important motive. You meet your soul mate in order to bring about systemic change on this planet. Inspired by your desire to share your love with the world, you and your soul mate will perform wondrous deeds that will contribute to the transformation of the consciousness of humankind. Put simply, when two soul mates find one another, their collective victory over selfishness weakens the forces of ego on the entire planet. By releasing a little bit of unconditional love into the spiritual atmosphere, you make it that much easier for others to triumph over the ego. In this way, your unconditional love affects and influences everyone else.

The Ultimate Payoff

Because the reward of loving unconditionally has been hidden away by design, we are afraid to put the needs of another ahead of our own. We fear we will wind up with less—or, even worse, with nothing. But the truth is, when an individual soul genuinely completes its transformation, thoroughly removing all the layers of ego and mastering the divine art of loving unconditionally, at that precise moment a curtain is pulled back. Suddenly unimaginable happiness, love, and joy are revealed in the lives of both partners. And the rest of the world feels it as well.

Even better, when the number of human beings who learn to love unconditionally reaches critical mass, another curtain will be pulled back, and the whole world will transform in that historic moment (more about this later on). Suffice it to say that the more layers of ego you eliminate, the greater your chances of meeting your soul mate.

Needless to say, the Opponent will use all his cunning to keep you estranged from your other half. It is in the Opponent's best interest to keep you two separate, because the moment you close the circuit of love, the energy you and your soul mate emit together will be awe-inspiring. Your combined Light will diminish the Opponent like a laser cutting through the darkness. It's no wonder that he works so hard to keep you confused and off balance!

BEAUTY AND THE BEAST

According to kabbalistic lore, some three centuries ago a very wealthy man lived in a small Russian village. This man had an incredibly beautiful daughter who was of marrying age. Men far and wide came to court the magnificent young lady and ask for her hand in marriage, but she refused to marry any of her prospects.

One day her father heard a knock at the door. He opened the door to discover a young man with a hunchback standing there expectantly. After speaking with the young man for a moment, the father discovered that despite his deformity, he was exceptionally learned and well spoken. In fact, he had come to ask for the daughter's hand in marriage.

The father could not contain his disbelief. He explained to the deformed man that his daughter had an endless supply of viable suitors. She would never choose a man with such an obvious physical flaw.

But the man at the door was persistent. He confidently told the father that he needed a mere five minutes to speak to his daughter. Out of pity for the young man, the father obliged.

After five brief minutes, the daughter ran up to her father and hugged him excitedly. She proudly told him that she had finally found the young man for whom she had been waiting. Her father was visibly shocked. Before he could ask what had transpired during their brief meeting, she explained to her father that she and the deformed man were two halves of one soul. She went on to tell her father some surprising news: According to the laws of karma and reincarnation, she was the one who should have been born with the physical defect, and not the young man who had visited her. In fact, her suitor had willingly made an arrangement with the Creator to spare her soul the pain and torment the deformity would surely have caused her.

In those five minutes, the two young people had seen through the layers of ego to the heart of each other's soul. It was then that they discovered that they were looking in a mirror, that they were two matching pieces of a divine puzzle.

Even though only a handful of us will earn the right to meet our soul mate in this lifetime, you shouldn't give up. Not for a moment. That's because the bigger picture is this: We are all soul mates; we are all parts of the same whole. You have soul mates in *every* aspect of your life; you are surrounded by people who, like you, were all pieces of the original Vessel.

The soul mates that show up in your life are there in order for you to achieve maximum spiritual growth in this lifetime. Everyone, from your boss to your child, shows up in your life to help you identify and overcome your most reactive traits. The job of those people, by virtue of their own behavior, is to trigger reactions within you so that you can come to recognize those faults and transform them into opportunities to share.

And you appear in the lives of others to do the same thing for them! So instead of finding ways to end a relationship with someone who pushes your buttons, view that relationship as a chance to grow spiritually. When you come to see your relationships in this light, you will realize that no relationship or marriage is ever a mistake. To the contrary, every relationship is part of a divine learning process—one that is leading you to endless happiness should you embrace it.

Just remember this: Every relationship is made up of two individuals whose souls yearn to be reunited. The divine glue that brings these souls together is unconditional love. The only way we can love like this is when we are in relationships with other souls.

Relationships give us that opportunity. (Read this ten times. It is simple but profound.) Without other souls, we can never re-create oneness. Without relationships, we could never learn how to shed the curtains of our ego and unleash our true nature—that spark of God—within us.

The way to love is through the ego—specifically through its elimination!

Chapter Four

transformation:
from *need* to *love*

REMOVING THE LAYERS

So how do you unearth the love within you so that you can share it with others?

You begin by identifying the individual layers the Opponent has created. These layers take the form of false pride, self-pity, fear, anger, self-hatred, intolerance, and insecurity, to name just a few. The following litmus test can help determine whether the ego is at play: If the emotion or feeling you're experiencing offers you a temporary sensation of gratification followed by emptiness or regret, you can bet that ego is hard at work.

Think of a time when you felt lonely, unloved, or abandoned, for example. When you feel like this, it is tempting to wallow in the feeling, thereby fueling more self-pity and isolation. That's precisely what the Opponent wants. In times like these, the Opponent uses false pride to convince you that you'll make it through, that you are strong, and that you shouldn't burden others with your loneliness. But these thoughts just promote more emptiness and isolation, adding another layer of obscurity. Your Light's beam appears even dimmer, and love begins to seem hopelessly far away.

Love Thyself

Self-hate is yet another tool of the Opponent. The Opponent dishes out insufferable attacks on your self-esteem to keep you from knowing your true identity. You feel as though you are a failure at love and life; you fret about your appearance, relationships, career, and future. This red herring keeps you busy with self-recrimination and shame, ending your journey to self-discovery before it even begins.

Rejection

Fear of rejection is closely linked to self-hate, and it, too, is grounded entirely in ego. You fear rejection from those who do not know you all that well, and you fear it even more from those who do. So out of fear, you with-hold your love. Or, conversely, you do everything in your power to provide for the emotional and physical needs of another with the singular hope that they will not reject you. When you choose to employ these ego-inspired defenses, you bury your love even deeper than before.

Fear, self-hate, pride—these are just a handful of tools the Opponent uses to distract and dissuade you from uncovering the Light within. But identifying these layers is only the first step; removing them is another task entirely. In order to eradicate ego, we must practice something called Resistance.

RESISTANCE AS A PATH TO LOVE

Beware the path of least resistance! The path of *most* resistance is the quickest path to love. It's important to note that resisting your reactive nature is not the same as suppressing your desires. Repression is a dead-end street; it only creates long-term physical and emotional stress. Ulcers, heart attacks, depression, high blood pressure, addiction, you name it—when you stuff down your desires and pretend that they do not exist, they inevitably reappear in another form. Resisting our impulses, on the other hand, is the first step toward revealing the love within. Resistance comes from knowing that the action will pay off in spades over the long term.

But there is a second, equally critical step. After you resist your nature, you must share your love with others. Yet the best ways to do that are not always apparent, because the Opponent is working hard to obscure them. So you must ask yourself, "Where are there opportunities to love in this situation?" When you open yourself up in this way to the wisdom of the Light, the answers will appear effortlessly. Remember that opportunities to share love exist in every situation.

Practice Makes Perfect

Your partner makes an insensitive comment, and your primal instinct is to react with anger or a hurtful comment. You practice Resistance by recognizing this impulse and choosing not to act on it. You accept the truth that a soul cannot be insulted, so it can only be your ego that is hurt. And a hurt ego is a good thing, for it allows your soul to shine brighter. Next, you must activate your sharing nature. Sharing your love might mean putting your arms around your partner when you don't feel like it at all, or choosing loving words when you'd prefer to use words equipped with barbs. In other words, instead of making this whole situation about your own ego (receiving), you make it about loving your partner (sharing).

Refusing Instant Gratification

Another example is saying no to a stranger who wants to take you home when you yearn for companionship, even if it's just for one night. By saying no, you are resisting momentary gratification that will lead to feelings of emptiness and regret. Instead, engage in an act of sharing by investing your gifts in relationships that facilitate lasting love in return—relationships that offer a true circuitry of fulfillment.

Parental Love

Practicing these two steps with your children fosters this same circuitry of love. You resist your desire to be abrupt with your child when you are in desperate need of quiet time, and then you share your love by explaining to your child in a caring way the importance of respect and compassion for one another's needs. You continue to share by setting aside time to enjoy their company, thereby revealing love together.

The two-step process of resisting and sharing takes practice. Practice, practice, and more practice—that is the only way you'll learn to resist your reactive nature and share your love. Resisting your base inclinations and activating your sharing nature is uncomfortable by divine design. If you are sharing and are deriving pleasure, it's not sharing.

Because it's uncomfortable, you will be tempted to bypass this two-step process entirely. What happens then? When you choose to indulge your desires by screaming in anger at your spouse or by saying yes to a stranger's advances, you'll receive brief pleasure, like a blinding flash of blissful light. But it will be followed by nothing, just as a short-circuit is always followed by darkness. The bottom line is that you can't take short cuts in removing layers of ego. The hard work itself is what reveals love and ultimately leads to true transformation—both for you and for those around you.

THE CANDLE MAKER

There was once a poor candle maker named Jacob who heard of a faraway island where diamonds were as commonplace as pebbles. According to Jacob's sources, the shores of this island were literally awash in the brilliance of the precious gems. So he packed his things, told his adoring family goodbye, and hopped a ship heading to the island.

When Jacob arrived, he discovered that the island was no idle rumor. It was covered with the glittering gemstones, and he began stuffing as many diamonds as he could into his bag. An inhabitant of the island approached Jacob and told him that he was wasting his time filling his bags with those worthless pebbles. Confused, Jacob asked why. The inhabitant explained that the ship that had brought Jacob to the island came only once every seven years, and that Jacob had better have a trade to keep him occupied until then. Jacob proudly explained that he was a talented candle maker, so the inhabitant encouraged him to get to work making candles.

Jacob did just that, and after seven years he was the owner of a successful candle business. But he missed his family dearly, so when the ship finally came back after seven years, Jacob quickly packed his possessions and jumped aboard.

When Jacob arrived home, his family was overjoyed to see him. They couldn't wait to see the bagfuls of diamonds that Jacob had collected. But to the profound disappointment of his wife and children, when Jacob opened his bags, they were filled with nothing but candles. There was not a diamond to be found. Their shock was palpable.

Jacob tried to explain that those very candles had made him an important man on the island, but he did not get far before he realized the profundity of his mistake—he had completely forgotten his reason for traveling to the remote island, and now he and his family were no better off than when he had left so many years before.

The sad truth is that we behave just like Jacob every day of our lives. Despite the fact that we are surrounded by innumerable opportunities to share our love, we take those opportunities for granted. We throw precious diamonds by the wayside or ignore them completely. We get caught up in the daily grind, desperately trying to fulfill our roles as parents, breadwinners, children, and friends while forgetting our ultimate purpose in life. Just as Jacob was given the opportunity to create profound change in his own life and in the lives of his family members, you have the potential every day to ignite a chain reaction that will transform the consciousness of humankind as we know it.

And this chain reaction all starts with one single principle . . .

LOVE THY NEIGHBOR AS THYSELF

You've probably heard this age-old wisdom since you were a child. It's a profound message that is both ingrained in our collective consciousness and completely ignored. How could that be? Perhaps the statement has become so overused that we are no longer inspired to look closely at its meaning and examine its far-reaching implications. But when we use the lens of Kabbalah, we see the significance of this statement in its magnificent, true proportions. When you know that we are all divine pieces of the very same Vessel, you realize that your neighbor, your loved ones, and even strangers on the other side of the planet are not separate from you at all. There is no division; there is no "me" and "them."

There is only oneness.

You and every other soul on this planet are inextricably linked; you are all parts of the same body. And just as you cannot cut off your own hand and spare the rest of your body the repercussions, you cannot withhold your love from another person without affecting the whole of humanity. A message of such critical importance could only have divine origins.

You now know that according to numerology, every written word has a pure, inherent meaning that is not influenced by interpretation. That said, biblical stories also contain an abundance of symbolic meanings embedded in the written words. We can use these stories as an extraordinary vehicle for exposing our true, divine purpose.

Deconstructing the Bible

Because the Creator desired to construct a perfect world in which we could manifest love by conscious choice, God needed to impart to humankind the necessary wisdom to make this goal a reality. God could have picked any number of recipients for this vital message, but a teacher by the name of Moses was chosen.

Why?

Moses had a community of people around him. In fact, Moses had hundreds of thousands of individuals at his side, whom he was leading away from slavery, away from the Opponent, and away from the whims of the ego. Moses was rescuing each and every one of the Israelites from their own anger, envy, impatience, low self-esteem, and greed. He was leading them away from the physical world of pandemonium and pain.

This wasn't just any community, and these weren't just any people. These individuals were ready and willing to accept responsibility for their actions and commit to generating a divine circuitry of love. Specifically, each one of the 600,000 souls agreed to let go of all self-interest and focus their efforts solely on fulfilling the needs of another. This sounds simple, but it's hard to grasp the profundity of this action. It works like this:

With every one of the 600,000 souls 100 percent committed and dedicated to serving their fellow man, it's easy for an individual to stop worrying about his own needs. Why? Because the individual can go to sleep at night secure in the thought that 599,999 other souls are worrying about his needs for him. Thus, the individual is free to focus all of his effort on serving others. He or she will lack for nothing, because all the other souls will provide this individual with everything he or she needs to be happy. This is why we need a nation: We have many needs, so we require many people to fulfill those needs. Each soul comes into this world with a particular talent, a set of gifts that were given to him so that he could share it with others.

But here's the potential problem: If just one person decides to hold back even a little bit—say, 10 percent —on his commitment to share unconditionally, that person affects the rest of the nation. How? In the depths of their souls, everyone else knows that they are missing something from the person who is now withholding. Suddenly, thanks to this absence, they feel a stronger need. This sets in motion a chain reaction of withholding that spirals out of control. The entire nation now descends into a state of receiving instead of a pure state of sharing. The magic is gone. Paradise is lost.

But Moses had the potential to sidestep this problem. He was the perfect candidate because he had the ideal environment in which to manifest the promise of this divine principle. He had a nation of people committed to the concept of Love Thy Neighbor. Still, the nation that Moses led out of slavery eventually stumbled and lost their consciousness. They blew it, and now it's up to us to regain it.

Just as Moses was the perfect candidate, so are you. You can begin to transform your community, your world, into the ultimate circuitry of love.

How do you achieve this?

Well, just imagine yourself as one of hundreds of thousands of dedicated people who make a commitment to love your neighbor as you love yourself. You would devote your entire life exclusively to sharing your love with your neighbor. You would never want for love, because there would be thousands of other souls who are devoting 24 hours each day to sharing their love with you.

On a practical level, it would look something like this:

If your neighbor were a plumber, your leaky pipes would be repaired for free. If another member of your community built homes, you'd be living in a sturdy, comfortable home. And if you happened to be a baker or chef, you would nourish your community with your hearty dishes and wholesome breads. You would never have to worry about finding a babysitter, and you'd never have to spend a moment wondering if you could afford next month's rent.

Everyone would be looking after everybody else. You wouldn't have to spend one minute trying to fulfill your own needs. You would be in a constant state of sharing, and your Vessel, your own spiritual storage unit, would be perpetually full of love. This interaction among neighbors, family, and even strangers would consist of simultaneous receiving and giving, creating a complete, unbroken circuit of love.

But circuitry such as this can occur only with your commitment to sharing the totality of your love. If you are not truly committed to resisting your physical nature and sharing wholeheartedly, it will have an inevitable ripple effect, affecting every member of society.

Remember that game where everyone stands in a circle and you face the back of the person in front of you? You stand a mere foot or so away from one another, and then you are asked to sit down. If everyone sits down simultaneously, the circle is completed by each person sitting on the lap of the person behind them. But if one person allows fear to rule their decision making and fails to meet their obligation, the circle is broken and everyone tumbles to the ground.

When you are playing the game, this result is pretty funny. The consequence of one person's mistake is usually just a bump on the elbow at worst and a hearty laugh at best. But in the real world, our failure to share our love leads to pain, chaos, and lack of fulfillment in our lives. It happens every day. It's happening right now, with your spouse, your partner, your friends, and your children. If you're sharing only part of your loving potential and are holding back the rest for yourself, your loved ones will respond by doing the same. They will withdraw their investment. When you are desperate to receive, you smother the love radiating from your soul—but when you commit to sharing your love without fear and hesitation, you become part of the perfectly functioning unit of giving and receiving. It begins with two people but extends to the entire world.

DECONSTRUCTING HEAVEN
AND HELL

There's a story about a man who talks to God about the difference between heaven and hell. God offers him a tour of both places, and the man graciously accepts the offer.

God takes him to hell, where he sees thousands of emaciated men, women, and children. Their misery is profound; they are desperate and starving. As the man looks closer, he notices a huge pot of stew in the middle of the famished masses. The steaming concoction smells exquisite, and it is loaded with the freshest meats and vegetables imaginable.

He also sees that every soul has a spoon tied to his or her hand. The handle of the spoon is so long and heavy that they are unable to bring the spoon to their mouths to eat no matter how hard they try.

God completes the tour by taking the man to heaven. In heaven, the man sees the same enormous pot of delicious-looking stew and the same cumbersome spoons tied to the people's hands. But here in heaven, each person looks well-nourished and robust. He asks God to explain the difference, and God prompts the man to look again. When he does, he sees that in heaven, the people have learned to feed one other.

We too can partake of the delectable Light forever, but in order to do so, we must learn to feed one another. We must love one another as we love ourselves. You taste of the Light when you give it to another and another gives it to you.

When you commit to this journey, a certainty, a knowing, will manifest itself within you. This certainty grows stronger as you share more love. You will begin to know at the core of your being that your need for love can be satisfied by the billions of people who share this planet with you. And you will recognize that by using your own God-given talents, you can share love without trepidation with all the souls who require it of you. You will experience, on a personal level, this ultimate circuitry of sharing and receiving that is true love. I believe that is why you picked up this book. This is what your heart yearns for. And realizing this love starts with you.

THE APPLE THIEF AND
THE SHOPKEEPER

There was a once a powerful king who ruled his king-dom with an iron fist. And with good reason. The vast majority of his subjects were a rowdy bunch. It was a dog-eat-dog existence, with each man out for himself. One day, a man by the name of Nathanael was caught stealing an apple from an apple-cart vendor. Now, you should know that Nathanael was not really a bad per-son. It wasn't really in his nature to steal anything from anyone. But after living among so many scoundrels for so many years, he simply gave in to his selfishness on this one occasion. He picked a bad time to make his first mistake.

The King was in a particularly foul mood because the crime rate had risen for seven straight days. The King knew he had to make an example of someone in order to send a message to the rest of the people—and so it was that Nathanael was sentenced to die for his crime.

The first-time bandit accepted his fate without any fuss. After all, he had no one to blame but himself.

The King asked Nathanael if he had any last request. He did. Nathanael asked if he could have three days to settle his affairs. Nathanael had to pay off some business debts, he owed a few personal favors, and he wanted to say goodbye to all of his loved ones. He figured that in three days, he could tidy it all up. The King was impressed by Nathanael's acceptance of his fate and his sense of responsibility, so he agreed to accommodate this last request. But there was an obvious problem. "If I grant you this temporary reprieve," the King said, "I have no assurances that you will ever return to fulfill your sentence." Nathanael understood the King's dilemma. "I have an idea," Nathanael responded. "Suppose I have a good friend stand in for me until I return. If I am late, you can execute my friend in my place." The King laughed. "If you can find someone who will take your place, I will grant you your three days. But if you are even one minute late, you can be sure your friend will be hanged on the gallows."

Nathanael asked his best friend, a shopkeeper by the name of Simon, to stand in his place. Simon and Nathanael had known one another since childhood. And Simon loved Nathanael like a brother, so he told his best friend that he would be honored to go into temporary custody on his behalf. Simon was handcuffed and detained while Nathanael hurried off to wind up his affairs. "Remember," the King yelled out, "one minute late and I will hang your best friend."

One day passed; then two more. Nathanael never showed up. He was one hour late when the King ordered Simon to the gallows, where he was confronted with the hangman's rope. A noose was slipped around Simon's neck. The hangman tightened it. A hood was put over Simon's head. And then, suddenly, a voice was heard screaming far off in the distance. "Stop! Stop! I have returned!" It was Nathanael. "Please, I beg you," Nathanael cried to the King. "Remove the noose from my best friend. This is my fate, not his." But the King replied, "You are one hour late."

Nathanael was so out of breath he could hardly talk. "You don't understand, Your Majesty. My horse became lame. I was forced to run all the way back. That is why I am late. It is I who should die, not my dear friend."

Suddenly Simon began to cry out. The hangman removed the hood from his head. "That is not true. I am the one who should die today. We had an agreement. Besides, I could not stand here and watch my best friend die before my eyes. Nor could I bear living without you. So it will be I who will die today."

Nathanael's eyes welled up with tears. "I beg you, Your Majesty. Do not listen to him. Do not let my best friend die. It is I who was originally sentenced to death, not Simon. If you kill him, I will not be able to live with the pain of seeing my dear friend depart from this earth. I beg you to take me." Simon and Nathanael continued arguing, and not surprisingly, the King was taken aback. In a land rampant with hooligans, the King was not accustomed to seeing acts of unconditional love.

Nevertheless, a decision had to be made, and justice had to be meted out according to the law of the land.

"I have reached a final verdict," the King said. "Today, neither one of you shall die. For I realize that if one of you dies today, I will be killing two men. The original sentence called for only one man to die. Thus, I am forced to set you both free."

"Love Thy Neighbor" Pays Off

The mind-boggling secret encoded in this tale reveals why one should love his neighbor and why an individual should put his enemy's interests ahead of his own: *self-interest!* Does that sound as if it goes against everything I've been saying? Keep reading.

Based on the law of the land, Nathanael was destined to die. But suddenly, after a few turns of events, Simon, his best friend, now found himself on death row. Think about it. Both men warranted death sentences, but both men avoided their fate because they let go of all selfish inclinations. They rejected selfishness and considered only the welfare of the other person. Unconditionally. No strings attached. Both men had become so tightly unified by their love and concern for one another that the pain of one became the pain of the other. Thus, if one man were put to death, two would die. The wise King saw this and was forced to cancel the decree of death, for it would violate the law that had determined that only one man should die.

This kabbalistic parable is telling us something quite extraordinary: We can defy the natural laws of the land, including the laws of physics and the fate of death, if we just share love unconditionally. Even more profound, genuinely putting the welfare of others ahead of our own *serves our own deepest self-interest.* All we need to do is strip away the greatest illusion and fraud ever perpetrated on the world. What is that illusion?

The Illusion

The only illusion we must overcome to find true love and happiness is the illusion that in order to receive, we must pursue our superficial, selfish impulses—to seek instant gratification.

Our Opponent has one function: to convince you that the story about the apple thief is just a nice, cute tale without any relevance or actual technology that can be applied in your life. And if you are completely honest with yourself, you will see that doubts and fear and skepticism are battling you at this very moment. How could you possibly behave like the apple thief or his friend?

The truth lies just where we expect it the least. When we master the ability to love another person unconditionally, without any regard for what we receive, the ultimate paradox occurs: We receive everything! You see, it's not about what you *get*; it's only about what you *give*. This is the ULTIMATE irony of life: When you give unconditionally, you get it all unconditionally. However, if you give in order to get, you will never get.

Only when you give for the sole sake of giving can you truly receive. It seems to be impossible. But it's not.

THE BASIS OF A LOVING RELATIONSHIP

A happy, fulfilling, and love-filled relationship can occur only if it's based entirely on spiritual principles and goals—specifically the principles and goals outlined in this book.

Love never appears at the beginning of a relationship, especially a soul mate relationship. Love is the reward at the end of the journey. It has to be earned. Discovered. Worked for. This happens through a gradual process of ego elimination and ever-increasing acts of sharing (remember, true sharing occurs only when it's difficult and uncomfortable).

But what about all those pleasurable feelings at the very beginning of a new relationship? Or when you catch sight of someone attractive and suddenly your heart goes pitter-patter? Those emotions are merely the results of infatuation. They wear off after a while. Soon they disappear.

Infatuation is a potent narcotic. It's easy to get hooked, and it's difficult to get clear of it. But infatuation is only about one thing—ego! It's all about your own needs, your own feelings, and your own pleasures.

However, when two people realize what life is actually all about and what love is all about, they can focus on helping each other grow, eliminating their own needy traits and focusing on the ultimate purpose of life—personal and global transformation.

How?

- By sharing with your partner when it's most difficult.

- By admitting all of your selfish traits.

- By working hard to fulfill the needs of your partner ahead of your own.

- By understanding that love is divine, that love is the source of all happiness, and that the only way to achieve this happiness is by sharing it 100 percent without any regard to your own needs.

Then and only then will you experience the fulfillment of a loving relationship—fulfillment so richly satisfying that you don't even dare to imagine it. Go ahead. Dare.

MORE FROM NATIONAL BEST-SELLING AUTHOR YEHUDA BERG

The Kabbalah Book of Sex: & Other Mysteries of the Universe

The world is full of sex manuals instructing the reader on the ins and outs of great sex, but these tend to focus on only one aspect, the physical mechanics. According to Kabbalah, the key to fulfilling sex lies in self-awareness, not simply technique. Sex, according to Kabbalah, is the most powerful way to experience the Light of the Creator. It is also one of the most powerful ways to transform the world.

So why doesn't great sex happen all the time in our relationships? Why has the sexual act been so deeply linked to guilt, shame, and abuse? Why do long-term couples lose the spark and get bored with sex? *The Kabbalah Book of Sex* provides a solid foundation for understanding the origins of sex and its purpose, as well as practical kabbalistic tools to ignite your sex life. This ground-breaking guide teaches how to access higher levels of connection—to ourselves, our partners, and to spirit—and achieve unending passion, profound pleasure, and true fulfillment.

The Power of Kabbalah

Imagine your life filled with unending joy, purpose, and contentment. Imagine your days infused with pure insight and energy. This is *The Power of Kabbalah*. It is the path from the momentary pleasure that most of us settle for, to the lasting fulfillment that is yours to claim. Your deepest desires are waiting to be realized. But they are not limited to the temporary rush from closing a business deal, the short-term high from drugs, or a passionate sexual relationship that lasts only a few short months.

Wouldn't you like to experience a lasting sense of wholeness and peace that is unshakable, no matter what may be happening around you? Complete fulfillment is the promise of Kabbalah. Within these pages, you will learn how to look at and navigate through life in a whole new way. You will understand your purpose and how to receive the abundant gifts waiting for you. By making a critical transformation from a reactive to a proactive being, you will increase your creative energy, get control of your life, and enjoy new spiritual levels of existence. Kabbalah's ancient teaching is rooted in the perfect union of the physical and spiritual laws already at work in your life. Get ready to experience this exciting realm of awareness, meaning, and joy.

The wonder and wisdom of Kabbalah has influenced the world's leading spiritual, philosophical, religious, and scientific minds. Until today, however, it was hidden away in ancient texts, available only to scholars who knew where to look. Now after many centuries, *The Power of Kabbalah* resides right here in this one remarkable book. Here, at long last is the complete and simple path—actions you can take right now to create the life you desire and deserve.

The Power of Kabbalah Audio Tapes

The Power of Kabbalah is nothing less than a user's guide to the universe. Move beyond where you are right now to where you truly want to be—emotionally, spiritually, creatively. This exciting tape series brings you the ancient, authentic teaching of Kabbalah in a powerful, practical audio format.

www.72.com

God Does Not Create Miracles. You Do!

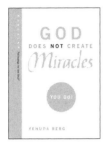

Stop "waiting for a miracle". . . and start making miracles happen!

If you think miracles are one-in-a-million "acts of God," this book will open your eyes and revolutionize your life, starting today! In *God Does Not Create Miracles*, Yehuda Berg gives you the tools to break free of whatever is standing between you and the complete happiness and fulfillment that is your real destiny.

You'll learn why entering the realm of miracles isn't a matter of waiting for a supernatural force to intervene on your behalf. It's about taking action now—using the powerful, practical tools of Kabbalah that Yehuda Berg has brought to the world in his international best sellers *The Power of Kabbalah* and *The 72 Names of God*. Now Yehuda reveals the most astonishing secret of all: the actual formula for creating a connection with the true source of miracles that lies only within yourself.

Discover the Technology for the Soul that really makes miracles happen—and unleash that power to create exactly the life you want and deserve!

The Red String Book: The Power of Protection

Read the book that everyone is *wearing!*

Discover the ancient technology that empowers and fuels the hugely popular Red String, the most widely recognized tool of kabbalistic wisdom. Yehuda Berg, author of the international best-seller *The 72 Names of God: Technology for the Soul*, continues to reveal the secrets of the world's oldest and most powerful wisdom with his new book, *The Red String Book: The Power of Protection*. Discover the antidote to the negative effects of the dreaded "Evil Eye" in this second book of the Technology for the Soul series.

Find out the real power behind the Red String and why millions of people won't leave home without it.

It's all here. Everything you wanted to know about the Red String but were afraid to ask!

The 72 Names of God for Kids:
A Treasury of Timeless Wisdom

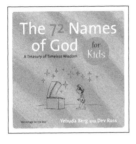

In often seemingly magical ways, the timeless philosophy portrayed in this book will help children overcome their fears and find their way to self-esteem, true friendship, love, and Light. The ancient secrets of Kabbalah revealed within these pages will give children a deeper understanding of their innate spiritual selves, along with powerful tools to help them make positive choices throughout their lives. The delightful, original color illustrations were created by the children of Spirituality for Kids who have used these universal lessons to change their own destinies. These are paired with simple and meaningful meditations, lessons, stories, poems, and fables inspired by the wisdom of Kabbalah.

MORE PRODUCTS THAT CAN HELP YOU BRING THE WISDOM OF KABBALAH INTO YOUR LIFE

God Wears Lipstick
By Karen Berg

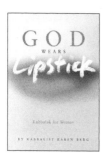

For 4,000 Years, Kabbalah was forbidden to women—until one woman decided that was long enough.

In directing Kabbalah Centres worldwide with her husband, Rav Berg, Karen Berg opened the world's most ancient form of wisdom to everyone on earth—for the first time.

Now, in *God Wears Lipstick*, she reveals women's special spiritual role in the universe.

Based on the secrets of Kabbalah, *God Wears Lipstick* explains the spiritual advantage of women, the power of soulmates, and the true purpose of life, and conducts a no-holds-barred discussion of everything from managing relationships to reincarnation to the sacred power and meaning of sex.

The Secret
By Michael Berg

Like a jewel that has been painstakingly cut and polished, *The Secret* reveals life's essence in its most concise and powerful form. Michael Berg begins by showing you how our everyday understanding of our purpose in the world is literally backwards. Whenever there is pain in our lives—indeed, whenever there is anything less than complete joy and fulfillment—this basic misunderstanding is the reason.

Wheels of a Soul
By Rav Berg

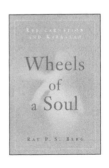

In *Wheels of a Soul*, Kabbalist Rav Berg reveals the keys to answering these and many more questions that lie at the heart of our existence as human beings. Specifically, Rav Berg explains why we must acknowledge and explore the lives we have already lived in order to understand the life we are living today . . .

Make no mistake: *you have been here before*. Reincarnation is a fact—and just as science is now beginning to recognize that time and space may be nothing but illusions, Rav Berg shows why death itself is the greatest illusion of all.

In this book you learn much more than the answers to these questions. You will understand your true purpose in the world and discover tools to identify your life's soul mate. Read *Wheels of a Soul* and let one of the greatest kabbalistic masters of our time change your life forever.

THE ZOHAR

"Bringing *The Zohar* from near oblivion to wide accessibility has taken many decades. It is an achievement of which we are truly proud and grateful."

—Michael Berg

Composed more than 2,000 years ago, *The Zohar* is a set of 23 books, a commentary on biblical and spiritual matters in the form of conversations among spiritual masters. But to describe *The Zohar* only in physical terms is greatly misleading. In truth, *The Zohar* is nothing less than a powerful tool for achieving the most important purposes of our lives. It was given to all humankind by the Creator to bring us protection, to connect us with the Creator's Light, and ultimately to fulfill our birthright of true spiritual transformation.

More than eighty years ago, when The Kabbalah Centre was founded, *The Zohar* had virtually disappeared from the world. Few people in the general population had ever heard of it. Whoever sought to read it—in any country, in any language, at any price—faced a long and futile search.

Today all this has changed. Through the work of The Kabbalah Centre and the editorial efforts of Michael Berg, *The Zohar* is now being brought to the world, not only in the original Aramaic language but also in English.

The new English *Zohar* provides everything for connecting to this sacred text on all levels: the original Aramaic text for scanning; an English translation; and clear, concise commentary for study and learning.

You can order these products from our Web site or by calling Student Support.

Student Support: Trained instructors are available 18 hours a day. These dedicated people are willing to answer any and all questions about Kabbalah and help guide you along in your effort to learn more. Just call **1-800-kabbalah**.

"Love Thy Neighbor As Thyself"

May we have the courage to go deep
within our souls to reconnect with
the unconditional love of the Creator

that exists within each of us.
By doing so and sharing that love,
we not only transform ourselves
but the entire world.